FLIGHT PATHS

POEMS 1979 — 2023

© Janet Upcher 2025

All rights reserved. Except for appropriate use in a book review, no part of this publication may be reproduced, stored in a retrieval system, or transmitted in any form or by any means, without the prior permission of the publisher, or in the case of photocopying or reprographic copying, a licence from the Copyright Agency of Australia.

FLIGHT PATHS

POEMS 1979 — 2023

Janet Upcher

ISBN 9781763825925

Walleah Press
South Launceston
Tasmania, Australia 7249
www.walleahpress.com.au
ralph.wessman@walleahpress.com.au

Walleah Press

FLIGHT PATHS

POEMS 1979 — 2023

JANET UPCHER

CONTENTS

I   1

Homecoming	3
Four Haikus	4
Bard	5
Earth's Creatures	6
Trinity	7
Owl	8
Marauders	9
Magpies	10
Discord	11
Sulphur-crested Cockatoos	12
Ravenous	13
Falcon	14
Masked Lapwing	15
Horse Power	16
Ravage	18
Skate	19

II   21

Sea Change	23
Transitioning	24
No Country for Old Trees	25
Widening Gyre	26
Sailing to Oblivion	28
Summer's Lease	30
Netting the Surf	31
Omens	32
Bosch Dreaming	33

III   35

Freight   37
Fragile   38
Mother Tongue   39
The Roast   40
Offcuts   41
Snag   42
Family tree   44
Romance   45
Nursery Rhymes for Newlyweds   47
Honeymoon   49
Kermese   50
Late Tarantella   51

IV   53

Worlds   55
Crossroads   56
Oxford Images   58
Flight Paths   60
Saskia's Gaze   61

V   63

Getting A Life   65
Naturally Yours   66
The Hairdresser   67
Nostalgia   68
Downsizing   69
Vignettes   70
Sundown   72
To Everything, Turn, Turn   73
Clouded   74

VI 75

Ascension	77
Metamorphosis (I)	78
Elegy	79
Scattering	80
My Lost Ulysses	82
Out, Out	83
Viewing Room	84
Metamorphosis (II)	86
Peace of the Heron	87
Acknowledgements	88
Previously Published Poems	88
About the Author	89

I

Homecoming

Is it simply
a traveller's heightened
awareness of place
that lets me see the light,
the space, the land,
the contrast of red earth,
green gum, blue sky,
that lets me hear
the sharp, stark sound
of the plover's cry
the pure clarity of a magpie's song
and the clear tinkling bellbird,
ringing nostalgia
like a gong?

Four Haikus

Paper Nautilus
Refugee from pounding surf
Rests in sand cradle

Flocks of silvereye
Flit among pink plum blossom
Green feathered olives

Huge helium moon
Mirrored in the glassy lake
A fisherman casts

Small bird sipping dew
The branch quivers with your weight
The tree breathes with you

Bard

From the moist earth
to cold unearthly twilight
softly sipping the nightfall dew
this small cicada comes.

Now, certain of his ground,
he strikes out Satchmo chords
in long pure sound.
Mysterious, mystical,
a strange and brittle music, mixed in silence,
mosaics from his lifelong upward journey
hammered and transmuted through the sky.

This enigmatic poet knows the fiery brilliance
at the centre of the earth,
the restless, teeming Heraclitean flux,
but thrusting ever upwards
from oblivion to truth,
confronts the constant paradox,
the dark night's stillness
at the moment of his birth.

In the quiet sky
one dying cadence rings,
yet somewhere still
mid counsellors and kings
a mild cicada sings.

Earth's Creatures

Damp earth moves
beneath musty leaf-litter.
Above the foliage,
midges and mosquitoes
drift on cooling air.

From a mound of soil
upwards through the earth
move multitudes of tiny insects.
Suspended between light and dark,
evening holds its breath.

From long years burrowing underground
countless small cicadas
crawl in columns towards trees
where they will sing and mate,
sprout diaphanous wings,
lay their eggs in bark,
and, having made new life,
hasten towards death.

Trinity

Silently at dawn they find the she-oak.
All day they stay perched on a low branch,
three squat sentinels, unmoving,
yellow eyes slanted half-shut
under tufted brows.
But for the occasional turn of a head
or shift of an eye,
they seem part of the tree.
Like revenants from ancient days
they watch, a tawny trinity,
feathers camouflaged, sad-mouthed,
blended into dark bark,
parents and owlet huddled,
a watchful trio roosting,
waiting for insects.
At dusk with drumming of wings
they rise and glide away,
leaving only an image, shadow-play.
Were they there or was it illusion?
Their silhouettes linger, silver-grey.
Spectral shadows flicker for days
in the foliage, bark-feathered frogmouths
vanished forever, transient as day

Owl

Feathery soft in the dark
poised like a question-mark
in the glacial sky
your wings glimmer
your eyes glow
with your tawny shimmer
and questing cry
you punctuate the night
of frost and snow.

Marauders

When the owl called at night
I flew with him in dreams
high over moonlit landscapes.
In swift sudden swoops,
we pounced on tiny creatures below.
At the quiet whoosh of our wings
there was scuttling, then silence.
We swallowed fur, tail and bone.
Surfing the sky until dawn,
I followed him home.

When I awoke in my room,
a baby rat stared wide-eyed from the floor,
whiskers twitching, tail trembling,
caught in my trap by his paw.

Magpies

Magpies trill their liquid stream
cascading, flowing from high in the tree
that bends and sways in heat and haze.
Day long, magpies ripple crystal pebbles,
a pure chorus, above arid croaks of crickets
and prickly cries of plover.
Their silky fluid song releases essence of summer,
sends showers of sound to drown
the drone of blowflies on dry parched air.
Warbling of magpies spills everywhere.

Discord

First it's the birds.
Some sudden disturbance.
They reel and whirl
beneath scudding clouds,
darting and diving,
almost colliding,
shrieking shrill, high-pitched cries.
Something's amiss in the world.
Something has stirred.
Birds are first to sense the upheaval.
Turning and wheeling in the darkening sky,
cockatoo, mynah and magpie
swooping and diving,
they screech and cry.

More eerie, the silence that follows.
What have they sensed?
Beyond bush, the sea is rising,
waves are dancing and leaping.
Somewhere, invisibly,
Earth heaves a sigh.

Sulphur-crested Cockatoos

Here they come, swarming,
storms of raucous marauders,
hell's yellow-splashed angels, avian raiders,
rasping the silence, clasping at bark,
shredding nuts, shrieking warnings,
shattering ear-drums and peace;
then the squadron scatters, disperses,
the raggedy mob, circling, reverses,
hoisting their crests, they hang tail-up,
like scraps of cloth from an op-shop
tattered white flags, truce or triumph,
victorious white feathers
in your stripped walnut tree.

Ravenous

Low overhead
swoops dark crow
in a slow loop,
encircling prey.

Harsh caws caaarrrk
like creaking doors
onto arboreal closets,
cold as confessionals.

Ragged raven wings
flap into bleak wind,
rushing, whooshing sound,
scattering leaves over dry ground.

Like stale breath
he hovers, cloaking the day
in mould and decay
gloating on meaty death.

A hobbling priest
in tattered black cassock,
swish-swish,
he alights to strike.

Hopping, one-legged,
he smites small beasts
croaks his excitement
boasts over glistening viscera.

Soon he retires, Brother Corvo,
to watch from great height,
satiate, remote,
he gloats.

Falcon

On draughts of air
he rides the sky, gliding,
hovering, sliding on wind.
Suddenly vertical,
across space, feet-first,
claws like rotor-blades,
he dives to snatch the frail
furred creature cowering
in the shade.
With his accomplice, air,
he takes the updraught
rides the thermal
back to his eyrie
back to his high ranch where
he spreads a feast of convoluted brains,
spongy lungs with branched veins
and long-skeined intestines
glistening in the sun.

Masked Lapwing

Stilted bird, stern-masked,
strutting stiff-legged on the highway,
fretting, searching, pining.

By night, she spikes the sky
with her cries
sharp and desolate as stars.

By day, gravely stalking her grief,
guarding her mate, a feathered mound
struck stone-dead by a driver.

Wandering relentless as clockwork,
wattles ruffled by wind,
helmeted, solitary, waiting.

How long her widow's vigil?
Will winter ice-over
Grief for her lost mating?

Horse Power

Walking the fields
at first light, I saw them,
five horses gleaming like bronze
in early sunlight,
guarding the newborn foal.

In a dew-damp field,
the tiny creature lay
struggling to stand, legs splayed
while five horses stood
sentinel still, scarcely breathing,
watching, waiting, unblinking.

At the fence, I stopped
intruder on a ritual.
The foal raised its head,
waved shaky forelegs in the air,
clambered to stand, then
lost balance, fell back again.
The stallion stamped his hoof,
the mare twitched her tail.
The other three stood frozen
silent, willing the foal to rise.

For almost an hour, mesmerized
I watched with the horses,
arrowed to the spot where the foal lay
frail, exposed in crisp dawn air.
The landscape sharpened its shapes.
And soon the hum of highway traffic
called me away, back to the
bustle, the drum-beat of another day.

I wondered how long a horse could stay motionless.
Those horses knew that soon it would happen.
The foal, needing no text to guide it,
would finally stand, as foals do,
its mother beside it.

Ravage

Rumbling like jumbo-jets overhead,
screams of fauna hurtling through bush
koalas and wombats, fur-balls on fire
echidnas, spikes alight like sparklers
trapped under trees flaring like fireworks,
swaying and flaming, ablaze and crashing.
Burnt humans clasping charred hoses,
shapes of their bodies scorched into ground.

Skate

In the glassy shallows of a quiet bay
a giant skate glides,
great underwater wings undulating,
imperious bird, gracefully pulsing up, down,
eagle of the deep.

Twenty years or more,
she's surveyed the bay,
cruising the shore,
making a monarch's claim to the shallows
at chosen times of day.

Too soon, netted by the local fool,
skate lies motionless
enmeshed in nylon, beached.
The net cuts deep, her elongated tail is still.
Her prehistoric eyes flicker, hollow, helpless.

See how the hero wades in his fishing gear,
armed with spade and club;
"Stand clear!" he shouts to children hovering near
then with a sickening thud,
embeds his shovel deep in skate's huge skull.

II

Sea change

That was the summer
of thunder and blood.
The first came with a warning.
Black sticky clouds clung
to the hills all morning
above the horizon,
above a sump-oil sea.

And then the sickening buzz
of the flies built to a pitch
in the thickening afternoon
along with the shrieks of gulls,
and the spiky cries of plover.

And then came the calm.
All the cicadas went quiet,
before the first crack of thunder,
the first dazzle of lightning, when
the sky seemed to burst, to split.

From inside the boatshed
she watched. By evening,
deeply bruised clouds blushed red.
From inside the boatshed
she waited. She wondered who knew
that dark sticky blood clung to her legs
and her bathers. How changed
seemed the sea, so changed.

A girl of twelve,
ashamed and shivering,
she hoped that others
in secret places secretly bled,
and they, too, had been caught by the storm.

Transitioning

Toads usurp thrones,
loathsome, grotesque,
controlling the world.
Mothers are barking
biting their offspring
baying at moonlight.
Dogs rule in kitchens,
pooches in aprons.
Owls fly by day
hopping among daisies
frogs leap among trees,
pouncing by night.
Earthworms slide above ground,
wilting, dying,
while cattle lay eggs
and chooks produce milk.
The sand turns black,
the sea ceases flotation,
the world turns backwards,
reversing rotation.

No Country for Old Trees

Seated on a stone, we survey
the valley, this vast forest.
Today, there's a rally to save the trees.
Beneath a regal stringy bark,
pods of pygmy politicians
huddle, nodding clockwork heads.
They have bonsaied their brains
through ignorance: to fell, or not to fell,
to burn, or not to burn.
And everywhere, every hill, every valley,
throbs to the march of machines,
their onslaught random and muddled
in a welter of felling and burning.
And everywhere youthful protesters
are yelling, imploring their elders to halt
the man-made destruction,
the smashing and hacking,
the trashing of beautiful natural things,
these large-limbed giants
whose defiant unhuggable trunks
so old, so old, outliving civilisations.
Stone-still on our seat, we watch
men in suits decide the fate of trees.
This is our age of progress.

Widening Gyre
(i.m. 9/11/2001)

Unaware, they fly on,
like falcons off-course,
flight-paths unknown.

Human hearts race,
hearts encaged in ribs,
ribs encaged in flesh,
flesh encased in seats
seats encased in cylindrical steel,
hurtling through space.

Time's last syllable
still unrecorded,
last desperate prayer;
What did they know or feel?

That steel would disintegrate
wings, hearts and limbs would
cremate in a crimson plume of flame,
descend to a great grey tomb?
Like moths to the candle drawn,
their masters of fate,
blazing eyes, hearts of stone,
crazed pilots, one purpose alone,
to ignite a blowtorch of hate.

****

The inferno dims to an eerie glow:
melt-down, a mound of dust and ash.
Love's lacunae leave cysts in a city's heart;
grief feeds on the swelling debris.

Steel beams squirm in metallic embrace,
where a simple black box slowly burns.
Night falls and the earth on its axis turns.

On the world's other side, at dawn we awake
to a sickle September moon and a star.
Is it only a paper moon
and could it be make-believe?

Sailing to Oblivion
(After W. B. Yeats)

A sultry Asian bay:
in a still harbour, body on body lay,
aboard a tiny, reeking boat.
All day in a scorching port,
the nameless, homeless, weak and sick
waited on a fetid deck.

When they left home, none knew the hell to follow.
The old, in one another's arms, the young,
with swollen tongues and eyes grown hollow,
had weathered sullen heat, torrential storms
and worse, the stagnant calms.

At last they neared Australia's shores,
Some cried and others sang.
They saw a ship approach; a naval flag
was hoisted, torn,
to greet them in the orchid dawn.
An officer embarked, a sailor
from their new-found land;
they welcomed him with outstretched hands.

"What right have you to stay?"
they heard his rasping voice.
"If you can pay to leave your shores,
we can't support your stay on ours:
we have no choice. This day, at noon,
(you've just six hours) we're sending you away".
With that, the envoy disappeared;
his brutal words rang terse and clear.
At length, a shrunken man stepped forward from
the creaking hull and crouched before the mast.
Slowly his words unfurled:

"This is no land for human-kind;
this boat's our world…we must sail on alone.
Alone we'll face what miseries there yet may be,
Across this sorrow-torn, this soul-tormented sea".

Summer's Lease

January's jam-packed with Eskis, jet-skis, and drones,
power-walkers stalking on board-walks with iPhones,
rock pools fetid with fish-guts, stinking dead cormorants,
feathers smothered in oil and bloated petrol-soaked petrels
floating in on high tide, cloaked in the debris of storms.

Each beach has its signs, pinpointing dangers
of faecal pollution, condoms, syringes,
U.V. radiation; swimmers are warned to leave nothing to chance.
Children are swathed in bright lycra, colours of Texta,
faces zinc-plastered, eyes blinkered, shaded from cancer.

Back then, the cries of the gulls could be heard
as they glided, guided by tides. The sounds
of oars on water lapping lulled us to sleep,
as the clipped plip and plup of balls
floated on airwaves, the pulse of our Davis Cup.

Nubile girls, bolder each year, picked pig-face
daisies for sandcastles, building their dreams,
watched by young boys, full of envy and scorn,
batsmen and bowlers, aiming for boundaries,
'maidens' and keeping the girls off their teams.

Back then, our honey-gold skins would peel, like
delicate mushrooms, great pale patches like bleach
on shoulders and shins. Smelling of Kwiktan,
tasting of seaweed and salt, we'd straggle back
to the shack, hungrily home from the beach.

Back then, the meat-safe buzzed with the drone
of blowflies, while magpies rippled the skies.
those were the days we had summer to share,
on our skins, in our hair. We floated
in bubbles of youth and danced on air.

Netting the Surf

Maybe today we'll go netting,
netting the surf for treasures too numerous,
voluminous, to mention. Perhaps we'll find
the usual dazzle of dinoflagellates dancing
in a bombardment of beer cans and sea-stars.
There's often a band-aid or two, floating
along with swabs from hospital waste,
and I swear, if we're lucky, we'll find
a swash of syringes and even, perhaps,
a plait of plastic six-pack packaging,
you know the ones, the kind
that dead, decaying cormorants wear,
encircling their necks, like amulets from the deep.
Sometimes too, if you care to look closely
among the stinking, decomposing bladder wrack
orphaned by tides, you'll find a different type of bladder
a silvery, gleaming thing, a beautiful, empty wine-cask,
discarded from some unknown yacht,
but not before the last drop has been drained
from its plastic tap, so often found (mistaken for molluscs)
lodged in the gullets of fairy penguins.
On special days, you might even spot a pod of dolphins,
wearing goggles and shearwaters with ringed beaks,
those rip-tops from cans make a pretty display
when tossed in a large, glittering pile through the foam.
But I think you'll agree, best of all,
is to see, as she slurps on the lip of the wave,
in the surf's crest and fall,
Mother-of-Pearl, a huge, sucking slick of oil.

Omens

I dream that I run by the harbour.
Overnight it's all changed.
Out of the mist
loom huge nuclear ships,
steel grey and menacing.
What we've been dreading
has somehow begun.
Where are my children?
Tucked safely in bed…
I run and I stumble
while "Ladybird, Ladybird"
wails in my head.

Bosch Dreaming

I dreamed the waiter prepared a platter,
severed mouse-heads, sun-dried to perfection
on fine pide bread, eyes opaque like whitebait,
whiskers stiffened like fish bones,
some slightly furred.

I dreamed a front-end loader
delivered dictionaries to shore up words,
like cracked clay, my arid word bank,
a kind of retaining wall
against your loss.

I dreamed our pet dog ate my still-born baby,
licked his chops in appreciation,
slurping on membrane,
final salivation
after Fido's last supper.

I dreamed of Christ, by association.
Armageddon arrived; the Messiah appeared
in robes and a nose-ring. Skate-boarding over clouds,
he bungee-jumped earthwards
for our salvation.

I dreamed our planet over-heated,
the oceans coagulated
in a thick ooze of plastic,
a huge viscous film
that cling-wrapped the world.

III

Freight

I lie in moonlight listening
to the beat of a boat, its steady chug-chug,
plying the river with an unknown load,
defying storm warnings,
engines forging ahead
into the wind
into safe harbour.

In semi-sleep, memory stirs
I hear the beat of the heart,
thud-thud of the blood
watch rhythmic lines on the screen
and imagine the child unseen,
a tiny being on maiden voyage
labouring onwards to an unknown port.

For months battling fogs, high seas and gales,
the freighter at last discharges its load,
delivers its burden to a welcoming port;
many hands wait to offload her cargo.

And after long months,
the mother discharges her load
into midwives' and father's waiting arms,
nine month journey for a tiny creature
ceaselessly afloat, swimming
towards this moment
to burst forth into their new world,
to bear forever the weight,
the freight of their dreams

Fragile

Teetering between life and death
you sleep in a humidicrib
blind to the fear in your parents' eyes
while they tiptoe on tightropes
of your cobwebbed breath.

Your eyelids flutter like butterflies
unsure on which side of the leaf,
which side of life to alight.
You are pinned under glass, under scrutiny
still not knowing day from night.

Mother Tongue

At three years old, my son is mastering
his mother tongue. New words are minted
fresh each day, most, slightly wrong,
but magically he's mimicking
the rules and managing to see
where parts of speech belong.
His eyes light up, as words, like wheels,
go rolling from his tongue.

My mother used to read to him.
She'd tell him nursery rhymes and fairy tales,
Little Pigs and Ugly Trolls
brought squeals of glee
to speed them on their garden strolls.

It is my mother now, at seventy-three
struggling to collect her words,
which suddenly, in one swift stroke,
have vanished overnight.
All momentum gone and locked in neutral gear,
she occupies a chair whose wheels are free to roll along,
unlike the ones that freeze behind her tongue.
The words won't move, but skid and stall and grind,
as if to mock the eloquence
inside her lucid mind.

The Roast

All the long week,
my mother mows the lawns,
cuts and carries wood,
weeds the garden,
heaves the shopping home,
along with baby and the dog.
And every Sunday,
she prepares the roast,
refills the gravy jug,
sets the table, warms the plates,
"three veg" (He mustn't starve).
And from His armchair, just on cue,
comes Father's voice:
"Leave the meat to me. I'll carve!"

Offcuts

Pigs' heads hang from hooks, bright blood leaks
from fleshy snouts on white lard stacked below in blocks.
Our butcher's boy, a red-head, in blue-striped apron
clutches his cleaver, clouting the chops
with never a glance at the meat on the marble slab,
chop, chop goes the chopper for obstinate bones like shin,
while a metal-toothed hacksaw gets to work
on stubborn forequarters, relinquishing knuckles from skin.

The butcher, wiping his stumpy hands
where a gobbet of blood has clung to a thumb,
wraps mutton chops in leaking paper
spread on the blood-stained bench
still glistening with entrails.
Just near the door stand twin steel pails
crammed to the rim with fleecy sheep's heads
and small cloven hooves swimming in sickly thick liquid like Bonox.

Back then, I couldn't wait to escape the steamy animal heat,
the frightful odours of offal, the meaty stench
and the bench-top's grisly stains.
Next door was the ragman's den and next door again
the thin clean green-grocer in the corner store,
his narrow aisles neatly stacked with packets of junket
and bright jelly crystals, cans of glinting sardines
and King Sound salmon. I loved to finger the leafy bunches of spinach,
green parsley, sage and mint
the feathery fronds of carrots and fennel, fresh in that cool retreat.

Early impressions remain, snap-frozen, uncut,
still life on storyboard, stained onto butcher's paper,
fixed in the frame.

Snag

She flies from kitchen to bathroom,
bathroom to bedroom,
all the while making toast,
stacking dishes, calling the children,
drying damp underwear, curling her hair,
putting the dog out, ironing the school clothes,
hither and yon, helter-skelter, gallop and grab,
rummage and run.
Meanwhile, he sits, plump as a duck,
puffed like a pigeon, nibbling and pecking
at muesli and Weet-bix,
chomping and chewing
on marmalade toast:
chomp chomp, gobble gobble,
reading the newspaper,
quite unaware
of the flurry and frenzy
that's happening elsewhere.
She looks at her watch
still in her night-clothes,
and ten minutes to go.
The lunches are done,
the children are clothed,
ready and fed.

She flings off pyjamas,
jumps in the bath, straight out again,
pulls on her costume without getting dry,
snags her new stockings,
brushes her hair, smudges her lipstick,
can't find her make-up, only odd shoes…
One minute to go.
He scrapes back his chair,
leaves plates and the paper still on the table.
"Goodness!" he cries, with a peck to her cheek,
"It's almost eight-thirty, I really must rush, it's best
to leave early at the start of the week."

Family Tree

"Money doesn't grow on trees," my father snarled
"we're in a credit squeeze".
So my pocket money halved.
Next day when he was out of range
I took the trusty tomahawk to prove him wrong,
and from the weeping willow's trunk, bludgeoned a wedge
to make a pocket for my coins, then stuffed them in.
The tree's damp flesh was raw beneath the gnarly bark.
My sixpences sat snugly in the hollowed space
where instant wealth would multiply within its hiding place.
The bark grew back: my deed went undetected.
For three months more I waited for my coins to sprout,
but then, a sudden lightning strike
cleft the trunk in two. I found no trace
of silver left, no shiny new-grown coins
within my niche, but just a stack of scattered limbs
and willow leaves. Too young to understand
my older brother's taunts of 'nouveau riche',
I felt bereft. I cursed my father and the tree,
nor could I keep from wondering why should
that willow weep, when it had cheated me.

Romance
"humankind cannot bear very much reality." (T.S. Eliot)

It didn't take long
        to discover
                the bluebird of happiness
is really a ragged moth
        beating its wings, fluttering over a sputtering candle,
        scattering ashes and dust.

It didn't take long
        to discover memory lane
            is really a thicket of thistles and brambles
                to snare the unwary
                    entangling lives in the present with lives from the past.

It didn't take long
        to discover the lover
            lurking way out in the wings,
      the prince on a trusty stallion,
                          is really a serpent,
                an asp with a poisonous sac
            to entice his bride
                    to a fantasy-land of milk and honey,
    a treacherous terrain, a stony battleground,
                romantically known as 'wedded bliss'.

It didn't take long
        to discover that the little bundle of joy
                is sometimes a squalling child,
                          violent and joyless.

But it took some time
      to discover how language deceives
           beguiling fools
      to believe that life is a cliché, a Hallmark greeting card
              filled with promised romance, melodies sweet,
        with notes rarely heard.

Nursery Rhymes for Newlyweds

"When will you pay me?"
Says the wife almost daily.
"Never, you bitch,"
Says the spouse growing rich.

*

Sing a song of housework,
A pocketful of pegs,
Four and twenty jobs to do
But Mummy has no legs.
All the gin is empty, the whisky jar is dry
And what can little children do
When Mummy starts to cry?
"Daddy's left the office,"
His secretary said,
"he won't be home till late, though,
so Mummy can drop dead!"

*

Hey diddle diddle
The poo and the piddle,
Mummy is cleaning the loos;
The kids are at play,
The dog's run away,
And Daddy is out on the booze.

*

Shop, cook, clean
Mummy's going to scream.
Splish, splash, splosh,
Mummy does the wash.
Hip, hip, hooray,
Daddy's gone away
Mummy cries all day
Now he'll have to pay!
Mummy's made a noose
"to hang a silly goose"…

Honeymoon

They ate, that night,
in a lamp-lit restaurant.
A crooner sang
'Isn't it romantic?'
Husband and wife
dining alone.
Nothing to say.
Faces of stone.
"Oysters aren't bad."
"Interesting wine."
"Do you think tomorrow
will be fine?"
Divining for words,
they chewed on chicken
and found the wishbone
already broken.

Kermesse

While you were dancing with wolves
I was washing nappies.
While you were shooting rapids,
I was doing dishes.
While you were leaving home in your suit,
I was still in my dressing-gown.
While you were the bread-winner,
I was the pudding-maker.
When you retire,
I will wear purple.
I will leave out your slippers
and foxtrot into the city
where I will waltz in winklepickers with hyenas.

Late Tarantella

Her life was a fretwork of wrong decisions
too long in the making.
She'd married Caution, old foe of the heart,
"just to be on the safe side".
He played his part, plotting
a carefully planned path,
performance indicators charting the trail.
And all the while,
she dreamed of a white village,
high in the Sierra,
flamenco, sangria, paella,
Spanish lover at dusk, a velvet-soft sky
and twinkling estrella.
But, to be on the safe side,
the dream was delayed;
instead, she stayed home.
The trail ended under the shade
of the dark verandah,
where swayed, from a nail
in the wrought iron railings,
a noose, loosely tied,
inviting tightening,
just to be on the safe side.

IV

Worlds

A snail in its fragile shell
drags along our garden rail.
Somewhere, perhaps in Paris now,
A small hotel yawns into day.
Are you stirring under laundered sheets
Or driving through the dawn-damp streets?
The snail leaves its tracery,
A silver slip-stream after rain.
Up there hangs a vapour trail,
A silver jet spurts frosted mist,
A metal cone compresses space,
Disappears without a trace.
I watch the delicate half-shelled snail,
Its whorled cosmology, tissue frail.
In two days' time you will be home,
today, a hemisphere away.
Are distances in time or space?
The world contracts to a snail's dome
And time expands to snail's pace.

Crossroads
(For my son, W.R.U.)

You are the son
grown to manhood.
You were the tiny bird
fluttering in the womb.
You were the small mammal
nibbling at the nipple,
the schoolboy who defied gravity
on a skateboard,
the student who glittered and flew high
and still you are flying.

Fly away, scholar,
a new universe, new university,
new hemisphere awaits;
you are crossing a threshold,
no turning back.
Your room is a hollow nest;
"If I don't come back, Mum,
you can sell what's left …"
And now, that hour at the airport,
Time's arrow takes aim at the heart.
You lean to me in a last embrace
choking a sob that crests in your throat
I feel the heave in your chest
the cleave in my own.
I think of all children leaving,
all mothers left in war and in peace.
"Boarding pass… you're together?"
"No. I'm alone."

Metal doors slide open,
my heart clangs shut.
Last clasp of the hand, the final cut
as you disappear behind steel.
Your after-shave lingers for weeks
like the after-blindness of love,
the after-numbness of grief

Oxford Images

A gossamer mist rises from the riverbank
wild irises tremble among the reeds,
fragrance of honeysuckle and old roses drifts on the air.
The morning sun rises low and full over the city
catching the gleaming spires of Christchurch,
the rosy tower of Magdalen.
Above the fields and woods beyond the towpath,
vapour trails crisscross the sky,
lipstick streaks ignited by sun.
Tracery of winter trees, skeleton branches,
soft light swirling from woods and streams,
where geese dapple the riverbank among the reeds
while ducks leave furrowed wakes.
Horses huddle in swirling mist
under a canopy of oak trees,
their breath blends with the foggy dew.
Mist swirls as ice crackles under foot
The brown Thames and Cherwell roll on beneath white ice;
ducks freeze there, motionless, snap-frozen for days
in this town, where oxen once crossed the ford,
where Vikings once arrived in hordes
where martyrs, Latimer, Cranmer and Ridley
once burned to death on Broad Street
as Elizabeth Tudor arrived in majesty
on horseback with courtiers
where today, in that exact spot,
with blue noses and purpling veins,
the homeless huddle with dogs
under the gargoyles of Magdalen.

Memorable still, these Oxford images:
Marston bike-track rolling through
white-powdered fields thick with snow-drifts,
ducks snap-frozen in the Cherwell,
icicles silently shining to the chill dawn
under a frieze of frosted fir trees
marking the sky-line
above cars strewn like random igloos
stranded, abandoned on Ferry Road

Flight Paths

Mist spirals from the river.
Swans paddle idly by
before take-off,
disappearing into mist, rising
on huge white wings.
Above, in labyrinthine shires of air,
silver metal wings trace flight paths
across hemispheres, across space
ascending, descending, never ending.
Now and then
a passenger stirs: a cough
a sigh, a child's cry
a rustle of blankets
above the whirr of engines
breaking the silence of endless sky.
All night in semi-sleep
we sail through galaxies,
thoughts and half-thoughts
drift among a sea of stars.
Meanwhile, swan, goose and owl
sail on by moonlight, silently
navigating avian air

Saskia's Gaze*

"Seeing comes before words." (John Berger)

Today he goes to Amsterdam,
sees sun-spun coins of gold across canals,
tulips bloom outside the Rijksmuseum,
church bells chime in echoing peals,
a painting, or a painter's poem.

Inside he finds a realm of men.
The male gaze: girls at windows, wearing pearls,
or women nude, like Bathsheba, frozen,
fixed in time, big-bellied; lustrous oils,
with glowing tones of lucent skin.

Such spacious chambers stretch ahead.
Sunday seems an endless trip through time;
portraits, landscapes, nudes, still life, staid
interiors of prim Dutch homes,
composed from lives long decomposed.

Transported through a dark-light world,
he comes across 'The Night Watch', feels the grief
reducing Rembrandt soon to rags, embroiled
in bickerings of bourgeois life,
male vanities he so reviled.

Saskia watches from a wall.
Her sickness cast a pall on final days.
Beloved wife, half-smiling, wears a veil,
spring-time bride, caught in the sun's rays,
watching him watching her, foretelling chill.

***

Sunday's light is fading now. Shadows knife
the walls, the air turns cold. He cannot go
until he asks: "Old mistresses and wives,
how did you see your men? Were there no
women painting then? No female eyes?"

Museum doors are locked and safe.
He leaves behind a darkened world of art,
dimmed as the eyes of an old Dutch Master's wife.
Outside, the sun's last slanting light
still yields warmth and calls him back to life.

*Saskia van Uylenburgh, Rembrandt's wife

V

Getting a Life

"I guess I'm a stay-at-home Mother," she said,
as her eldest left home with a toss of his head;
bit of a tear-away, bit of a lad,
(radical thinker, seeks a new pad)
"Take care please, mum, and don't ever lose
your freedom or interests…go on a cruise…"
(goodbye to the box-pleated skirt and flat shoes)
"Some day I'll be back, but it's freedom I seek!"
Soon her younger son left, with a peck to her cheek:
"Don't stay in a rut, mum, there's much to be done!"
so her heart was snap-frozen; they'd put out her sun.

One went into commerce, was elected Lord Mayor,
went on to big things and cut short his hair.
The other, a preacher, was saving mankind,
worked with the ageing, helping the blind.
Well, a few years went by, she turned sixty years young.
How changed seemed the world! It was time to have fun!
She took a grip on herself, began a new life,
she took up gymnastics, to keep out of strife,
started dressing in lycra, runners and tights
bought a new wet-suit and other delights.

She tried scuba-diving and kayaking, too;
sixty years on and so much to do,
sixty years on, just beginning the fun,
when soon, unexpectedly, home came her young!
"You're very left-wing, mum and what's with the hair?
And as for the tights, mum, how do you dare?"

"Well, red hair is chic, now, didn't you know?
And as for the tights, there's not much to show!
Besides my appearance, what else is new?
And where's your bandana, long hair and tattoo?
I've dared to be different - what's happened to you?"

Naturally Yours

I'm a pig-hearted girl (I've the valves of a hog)
and my liver, it's true, has come from a dog
(wild though, not tame — I've forgotten its name).
I do have a lung that isn't my own
(and some veins and some hair and part of a bone)
my lung's from an ox, my veins from a rabbit
my hair's all pure fox — I'm foxy by habit.
Though my face has been lifted, it's basically mine
(it looks slightly different, but much more refined)
my brain is a sheep's, and let it be said,
there's nothing quite like an old woolly head.
But now for my secret; the truth lies therein,
I've actually managed to save my own skin.
A transplant of conscience is all that I need.
A 'made-over me'? It's what glamour decreed.

The Hairdresser

My hairdresser has far too much to say:
"So hello, darling, how are we today?"
That really grates as I arrive, but soon:
"What are we having done this afternoon?"
Most often I'm inclined to say: "Just cut!"
But then he counters this: "You're in a rut..
You should get out more...get out and have a lark!
You're looking like some throw-back to the ark!"
And off he trots, with a toss of his head
to irritate some trendier client instead.
Returning, as it suits his whim and mood,
he sets to work, now calmer and less rude:
"Now, darling, have we thought about a style?"
"A silent one", I plead, with sweetest smile.

Nostalgia

I used to think I was young, once.
I'm afraid it's no longer so.
There used to be songs I'd have sung once,
In a voice quite sexy and low.

I used to be quite a wild child once
With my neckline plungingly low
But now I wear collars and buttons,
Fastened as high as they'll go.

I used to be fast as a foxtrot, once,
Dancing and prancing for show,
But these days, it's true, my legs
And my brain are quite impossibly slow.

I used to go out on adventures once
Seeking knowledge most ladies don't know
But now a trip to the bus-stop
Is as far as I'm likely to go.

I used to have skin like a peach, once,
But now I've skin like a crow.
I used to have curves and a figure, once
But now I'm the same, head to toe.

I used to be brazen and forward, once
With the boldness and nerve of a pro;
Now all my partners are parted or spent,
I guess, as you reap, so you sow.

If you thought I might have been rich, once
And that this is my tale of woe,
Then pass round the hat and the wallet,
To help an old lady's cash flow.

Downsizing

'Compact and tidy, little work to be done…'
A bit of a contrast to how they'd begun,
in a harbour-side mansion, facing the sun.

When the children moved out, left so much room,
echoing hallways, a house filled with gloom,
gathering dust and more like a tomb,

they sought a small place,
with just enough sun and minimal space,
carpets of shag-pile, curtains of lace.

Separate bedrooms, only one stair,
easily accessed by mother's wheelchair
but after a year, she needed more care.

Time to move on — into a hospice, a new kind of home,
barely the basics, but a room of one's own,
unable to move, nowhere to roam.

Next move more final. No work to be done,
under the gumtrees, sheltered from sun,
a polished container of walnut, brand new,
interred on an incline, a tomb with a view.

Vignettes

Eccentricity
He puts to sea in an umbrella;
walking out in the rain
with a boat on his head.

Old woman feeds peanuts
to passing cats; she takes Kitty Litter
to monkeys in the park.

Loneliness
Trapped between skyscrapers,
A lone seagull wheels, swoops, weaves through traffic
while the flock shelters behind sand dunes.

A small girl crouching grave-side
strews marigolds and daisies;
it's the day they call 'Mothering Sunday'.

Solitude
A black swan paddles solo
into the wind; a dog's plangent howl
rings out on a frosty night.

A single sock hangs on the Hill's Hoist;
a solitary shoe tossed by the roadside;
toast for one on Christmas day.

Old Age
Lavender soap, a gift from great-nieces,
curtains closed to keep in the grey;
the canary is losing its feathers.

Opulence
Business men amass empires,
wives amass acres of matching flesh;
excess baggage: surcharge is death.

Sundown

All day, hunched in the shade of her dark verandah,
watching the park where children play,
her gums work noiselessly, and she rocks herself
in her wicker chair, far, far away,
keeping silent time with the ticking clock
and the caged canary by her side.
At dusk, the children disappear.
She waits till their lingering laughter dies;
nothing more now can she hear.
When the park is still, she stoops inside,
as the sun slopes behind the hill.
And now, when last light's gone,
she sets again her single place,
a faded cloth where cold tea and crusts
remain since breakfast. Alone again,
she sits to taste silence on toast.

To Everything, Turn, Turn
(i.m. my mother, E.O.W.)

For seventy years she nursed us,
cajoled, cared for us, cursed us.
Now, as she lies, her small head
more pallid than the pillow,
it is her family's turn to nurse,
our chance to reverse and revoke
the pattern, ravelled through the years.

But on this hot night, helplessness is born.
We droop forlorn, like the willow
in shadow of the seasoned oak.
Storms rage and foliage is torn;
we cannot hide our fears.
And in high summer,
we shed winter tears.

Clouded

When I was small
I saw shapes in clouds,
more real than anything;
out of nowhere
clouds filled with dread
and hope, constantly changing,
my childhood kaleidoscope.
The silver-lined zeppelin
hovered over the mountain.
Elephant, lion and bear
stalked the skies, roaming in storms.
Tiger, shark, tusked pig and walrus
harrowed my girlhood heaven.

Serpent and devil came later.

I tend to look earthward now.
Walking alone on a beach,
shell, stick and stone,
a strand of seaweed or hair,
orphaned by tide
eddying memories.
A set of yellowed sheep's teeth,
feather and leaf, shell and bone,
exist beyond speech.
And always there's yearning,
wanting more than the visible,
searching for metaphor,
seeking the patterns connecting
creation, with meaning always
just out of reach.

VI

Ascension
A sonnet for Boxing Day, 2008
(i.m. my sister, R.E.B)

In those last hours, you found a curious peace,
stillness beyond what we could understand.
All through the night, your life-force slowly ceased:
no response…nothing when we squeezed your hand.
You'd used up all your strength on Christmas Day
in order not to spoil the children's fun
but when at night you drifted far away,
our hopes had gone, your end had just begun.
At dawn, some messenger had tapped upon
the pane: no angel, but a small grey bird
which made you rise, as though all pain had gone.
Your eyes shone bright as if a spirit stirred.
You sighed before one final sip of breath,
your feather spirit fluttered, freed by death.

Metamorphosis (I)
(i.m. my sister, R.E.B.)

I awoke
dreaming you'd become
a beautiful shimmering bird
in olive-green brocade;
your long, spangled tail
half mermaid or angel,
curling, dangling,
brightly feathered,
slightly scaled.
You nestled there
in the crook of my arm
gentle, splendid, rare
silently, slowly settling;
You whispered, "it's simply a word, 'dead'…"
Then, your song still to be heard,
you nodded your soft head,
and faded in the dim-lit air,
a beautiful, shimmering bird.

Elegy
(i.m. my sister, R.E B.)

She wanted few flowers at her funeral,
no soppy words at the start,
just something rare and exotic
something reflecting her art
like the luminous horn of a unicorn
or a tooth from Saint Joan of Arc
maybe a gargoyle from Notre Dame
or some stardust snatched from the dark
nothing silly or insincere
just something straight from the heart.

Scattering
(i.m. my sister, R.E.B)

The bay smiles, lucent under setting sun.
    We walk the length of the day's burden
        noticing how lichen clings to rocks
            turning them golden.
    We hear with new ears the suck and sigh of the tide;
        the tide also is turning.

There's a softness, a stillness in the air.
    Salt pungency of kelp
        stings our nostrils,
            eyes glisten.
    Everything seems heightened, listening,
        even the cries of gulls are keener.
    Who ever thought that ash
        might weigh so much?

Along the shore we carry you,
    heavy oblong shape, compacted in a box
        this *you,* our family brick.
    From its outlet, you're poured
        like powder snatched by wind,
            you drift on air
                not white like talcum
            nor petals floating –
                but grey like dust, or soot
        sifting into this small vessel
papier-mache, home-made, dusky pink,
        daughter-crafted, ship-shaped.

From these rocks, you're cast adrift.

       The sea is calm.
               Strewing yellow roses,
          (you loved all roses) we push you out to sea.
You sail onwards, to what coast?
                 In your cradle, tiny, now, crepuscular
                     delicate pellet, you float, lost
between sea and sky, swept from earth
        in fiery feathered sunset
                       to some far horizon,
             where all elements meet.

My Lost Ulysses
(i.m. my son, J.E.U)

In the dream
I had come to a place I know well,
yet in my dream it was unfamiliar.
I was searching for you
but I was lost in a tangle of alleyways.
You were lost too.
We were separated by a web of lanes, blind alleys
at strange angles driving us further apart.
After a steep descent over cobblestones
I arrived in a foreign port.
Fishmongers were yelling in strange tongues
bullying to buy their smelly catch.
A rank stench of diesel mixed with fish guts
drenched the dank air.
Cranes were winching containers onto vessels
waiting to depart.
I thought you were somehow trapped
in one of the sealed containers.
I threw myself from the wharf
just as you disappeared into the steel hold.
Your ship set sail; I floundered, flailing arms, wailing.
When I awoke, I was still lost, submerged,
Searching, drowning…

Out, Out
(After Robert Frost)
(i.m. my son, J.E.U)

The worst thing was not
finding your white breakfast bowl
laid out to drain in your sink.
It was not the worst thing
to find your groceries
all neatly stacked in your cupboard.
Nor was the worst thing seeing fresh milk
in the fridge and a chicken defrosting
ready for dinner when you returned.
It was almost the worst thing
seeing the mark on the floor
where you'd fallen after you tripped
and plunged to the foot of the stairs
breaking your neck on the way
blindly down in the dark.

No, the worst thing was
seeing you laid out and cold
in a hospital morgue
white, like the breakfast bowl
in your sink, cold as porcelain,
life, like water, drained away

Viewing Room
(i.m. my son, J.E.U)

I watched you that December day
snug in your crib in the Maternity Ward.
Among all babies, the sun shone only on you.
My heart swelled with pride as they lifted you for us to see.
'Unto us a boy is born' rang out with Christmas carols,
you, our first-born, *'king of all creation'*, our ode to joy.
Your eyes were closed, your skin, velvet,
your shell-shaped ear, pink and perfect.
Impatiently, your mouth opened and shut,
bird-like. Your feather-down hair smelled of milk.
You, my tiny peach, more like a small, round wren
fluttering at my breast,
our two hearts beating each to each.
You were the magnetic centre of the world.
The mystery and miracle of birth.

Thirty-seven years ago.
Today you're in another viewing room, another hospital,
A distant world, as far away as hope.
Like a bird bereft, I've flown with amputated wings
across two hemispheres to bring you home,
our lives forever lost, off course, no compass, no direction.
Your eyes are closed, you can no longer feel.
You lie like a bird with a broken neck, a fledgling fallen to earth.
Your skin is blotched, magenta. I kiss your face, cold like putty.
I try to hold your hands concealed beneath blue velvet,
candles burn in the dim-lit room, ethereal, other-worldly.
'The stars in the bright sky looked down where he lay'…

I stroke your arm, icy, heavy like alabaster
pale like plaster. Your lips are swollen, silent.
In your bruised, discoloured ear, I speak softly but you cannot hear.
Only your hair appears unchanged; it still retains your smell.
Desperately I call you but still you cannot hear.
My tears stain your face.
'Come and behold him'.
I want so much to hold him.
The chaplain asks: "Is there nothing I can do?"
My heart clamps. I close the door. Cramp in the chest.
The mystery and misery of death.

Metamorphosis (II)
(i.m. my son, J.E.U)

Today at the cemetery
you came as a butterfly
alighting on flowers
placed on your grave.

Yesterday you came as a magpie.
Close you came to my hand
sensing my despair
then you cocked your head,
opened your magpie beak
in full-throated song
as if in consolation,
as if you knew.

How will you come,
what will you be
tomorrow?

Peace of the Heron
(After Wendell Berry)

When wars, woes and weight of the world
wear you down, make for still waters,
find a lake or a river, find the white-faced heron
who stands patiently on the shore,
waiting for peace, for sunlight,
unaware of the turmoils of war
wanting nothing more
than food to sustain him in flight,
shelter to keep him alive:
his solitary fight, just to survive.

ACKNOWLEDGEMENTS

I am deeply indebted to my editor, Eliza Burke, who has curated my work which dates from the last three decades. With an astute understanding, perception and vision, she has prepared this manuscript. To the various journals in which my work has appeared, I am grateful. Similarly, I express thanks to those organisations which have conducted competitions in which I've received awards and recognition. The vibrant Tasmanian literary community, including FAW Tas., the Tasmanian Writers' Centre and Oasis Women's poetry have been very supportive and to them, I owe thanks. Ultimately, I thank my family, especially my two sons for their encouragement and always honest critical appraisal and support over the years. And my husband for enduring the moods of a temperamental and sometimes melancholy writer. Lastly, a word to honour the energy and professionalism of Ralph Wessman at Walleah Press who has helped and supported so many writers: I thank him especially for empowering *Flight Paths* to become airborne.

PREVIOUSLY PUBLISHED POEMS

'Earth's Creatures' *Quaternity*; 'Trinity' (published as 'Frogmouths'), 'Magpies' (published as 'Magpie Music', 'Homecoming' and 'Masked Lapwing' in *Birdsong, A Celebration of Bruny Island Birds 2021;* 'Owl' *Lip Service;* 'Three Horses' *Quicksilver Water*, Oasis Women Poets, 2022; 'Discord' *Turbulence and Shadowed* (self-published); 'Sea change' *Chautauqua Literary Journal,* (USA) 2004; 'Summer's Lease' *Tarralla*, (5), Tarralla Writer's Group, 2006; 'Bosch Dreaming' (published as 'A Net of Hands') *FAW Tas*, 2020; 'Mother Tongue' *Poetrix*, Western Women Writers, 2005; 'Nostalgia' and 'Late Tarantella' *Island Magazine* (95), 2003; 'Saskia's Gaze' *Island Magazine* (106), 2006; 'Honeymoon', *Australian Book Review,* 2007; 'Worlds' and 'Kermesse' *The Canberra Times* (ACT), 1997; 'Crossroads' Grieve, Hunter Writer's Centre, 2014; 'To Everything, Turn, Turn' *Southern Review,* 1979; 'Ascension' (published as 'When the World is New') 1st prize, Victorian Arts Cancer Council Award and *FAW Tas,* 2020.

ABOUT THE AUTHOR

Janet Upcher lives in Opossum Bay, near Hobart. She has travelled in the UK and Europe, has taught in Tasmania, East Timor and France, and writes anywhere. Although her favourite genre is poetry, she has published and won awards for short fiction, drama scripts, essays and reviews.

Alongside publishing her work in various journals, she has published longer works in diverse fields, including literary criticism, a history of Masters Athletics and collaborations with visual artist Jennifer Marshall to produce three Artist's books.

After teaching English Literature, English and French language at several Tasmanian tertiary institutions and pre-tertiary colleges and secondary schools, she retired to focus on being mother, editor, writer and reviewer.

She is now a devoted grandmother, beachcomber and bird watcher.

www.ingramcontent.com/pod-product-compliance
Ingram Content Group UK Ltd.
Pitfield, Milton Keynes, MK11 3LW, UK
UKHW040733190225
455309UK00004B/268